**HowExpert**

# How Write a Poem

## Your Step By Step Guide To Writing Poetry

**HowExpert**

**Copyright HowExpert™**
www.HowExpert.com

**For more tips related to this topic, visit HowExpert.com/poem.**

# Recommended Resources

- HowExpert.com – Quick 'How To' Guides on All Topics from A to Z by Everyday Experts.
- HowExpert.com/free – Free HowExpert Email Newsletter.
- HowExpert.com/books – HowExpert Books
- HowExpert.com/courses – HowExpert Courses
- HowExpert.com/clothing – HowExpert Clothing
- HowExpert.com/membership – HowExpert Membership Site
- HowExpert.com/affiliates – HowExpert Affiliate Program
- HowExpert.com/writers – Write About Your #1 Passion/Knowledge/Expertise & Become a HowExpert Author.
- HowExpert.com/resources – Additional HowExpert Recommended Resources
- YouTube.com/HowExpert – Subscribe to HowExpert YouTube.
- Instagram.com/HowExpert – Follow HowExpert on Instagram.
- Facebook.com/HowExpert – Follow HowExpert on Facebook.

# Publisher's Foreword

Dear HowExpert reader,

HowExpert publishes quick 'how to' guides on all topics from A to Z by everyday experts.

At HowExpert, our mission is to discover, empower, and maximize talents of everyday people to ultimately make a positive impact in the world for all topics from A to Z...one everyday expert at a time!

All of our HowExpert guides are written by everyday people just like you and me who have a passion, knowledge, and expertise for a specific topic.

We take great pride in selecting everyday experts who have a passion, great writing skills, and knowledge about a topic that they love to be able to teach you about the topic you are also passionate about and eager to learn about.

We hope you get a lot of value from our HowExpert guides and it can make a positive impact in your life in some kind of way. All of our readers including you altogether help us continue living our mission of making a positive impact in the world for all spheres of influences from A to Z.

If you enjoyed one of our HowExpert guides, then please take a moment to send us your feedback from wherever you got this book.

Thank you and we wish you all the best in all aspects of life.

Sincerely,

BJ Min
Founder & Publisher of HowExpert
HowExpert.com

PS...If you are also interested in becoming a HowExpert author, then please visit our website at HowExpert.com/writers. Thank you & again, all the best!

**COPYRIGHT, LEGAL NOTICE AND DISCLAIMER:**

COPYRIGHT © BY HOWEXPERT™ (OWNED BY HOT METHODS). ALL RIGHTS RESERVED WORLDWIDE. NO PART OF THIS PUBLICATION MAY BE REPRODUCED IN ANY FORM OR BY ANY MEANS, INCLUDING SCANNING, PHOTOCOPYING, OR OTHERWISE WITHOUT PRIOR WRITTEN PERMISSION OF THE COPYRIGHT HOLDER.

DISCLAIMER AND TERMS OF USE: PLEASE NOTE THAT MUCH OF THIS PUBLICATION IS BASED ON PERSONAL EXPERIENCE AND ANECDOTAL EVIDENCE. ALTHOUGH THE AUTHOR AND PUBLISHER HAVE MADE EVERY REASONABLE ATTEMPT TO ACHIEVE COMPLETE ACCURACY OF THE CONTENT IN THIS GUIDE, THEY ASSUME NO RESPONSIBILITY FOR ERRORS OR OMISSIONS. ALSO, YOU SHOULD USE THIS INFORMATION AS YOU SEE FIT, AND AT YOUR OWN RISK. YOUR PARTICULAR SITUATION MAY NOT BE EXACTLY SUITED TO THE EXAMPLES ILLUSTRATED HERE; IN FACT, IT'S LIKELY THAT THEY WON'T BE THE SAME, AND YOU SHOULD ADJUST YOUR USE OF THE INFORMATION AND RECOMMENDATIONS ACCORDINGLY.

THE AUTHOR AND PUBLISHER DO NOT WARRANT THE PERFORMANCE, EFFECTIVENESS OR APPLICABILITY OF ANY SITES LISTED OR LINKED TO IN THIS BOOK. ALL LINKS ARE FOR INFORMATION PURPOSES ONLY AND ARE NOT WARRANTED FOR CONTENT, ACCURACY OR ANY OTHER IMPLIED OR EXPLICIT PURPOSE.

ANY TRADEMARKS, SERVICE MARKS, PRODUCT NAMES OR NAMED FEATURES ARE ASSUMED TO BE THE PROPERTY OF THEIR RESPECTIVE OWNERS, AND ARE USED ONLY FOR REFERENCE. THERE IS NO IMPLIED ENDORSEMENT IF WE USE ONE OF THESE TERMS.

NO PART OF THIS BOOK MAY BE REPRODUCED, STORED IN A RETRIEVAL SYSTEM, OR TRANSMITTED BY ANY OTHER MEANS: ELECTRONIC, MECHANICAL, PHOTOCOPYING, RECORDING, OR OTHERWISE, WITHOUT THE PRIOR WRITTEN PERMISSION OF THE AUTHOR.

ANY VIOLATION BY STEALING THIS BOOK OR DOWNLOADING OR SHARING IT ILLEGALLY WILL BE PROSECUTED BY LAWYERS TO THE FULLEST EXTENT. THIS PUBLICATION IS PROTECTED UNDER THE US COPYRIGHT ACT OF 1976 AND ALL OTHER APPLICABLE INTERNATIONAL, FEDERAL, STATE AND LOCAL LAWS AND ALL RIGHTS ARE RESERVED, INCLUDING RESALE RIGHTS: YOU ARE NOT ALLOWED TO GIVE OR SELL THIS GUIDE TO ANYONE ELSE.

THIS PUBLICATION IS DESIGNED TO PROVIDE ACCURATE AND AUTHORITATIVE INFORMATION WITH REGARD TO THE SUBJECT MATTER COVERED. IT IS SOLD WITH THE UNDERSTANDING THAT THE AUTHORS AND PUBLISHERS ARE NOT ENGAGED IN RENDERING LEGAL, FINANCIAL, OR OTHER PROFESSIONAL ADVICE. LAWS AND PRACTICES OFTEN VARY FROM STATE TO STATE AND IF LEGAL OR OTHER EXPERT ASSISTANCE IS REQUIRED, THE SERVICES OF A PROFESSIONAL SHOULD BE SOUGHT. THE AUTHORS AND PUBLISHER SPECIFICALLY DISCLAIM ANY LIABILITY THAT IS INCURRED FROM THE USE OR APPLICATION OF THE CONTENTS OF THIS BOOK.

**COPYRIGHT BY HOWEXPERT™ (OWNED BY HOT METHODS)**

**ALL RIGHTS RESERVED WORLDWIDE.**

# Table of Contents

**Recommended Resources** ............................ 2
**Publisher's Foreword** .................................. 3
**Introduction** ................................................ 6
  *Notes on How to Use This Guide* ............................ 6
**Tools Of The Trade** ....................................... 8
  *1. Select a Notebook* .................................................. 8
  *2. Select a Writing Implement* ................................. 9
  *3. Get a Dictionary & Thesaurus* ............................ 10
  *4. Get a Poetry Anthology* ....................................... 11
**How To Write a Poem** ................................ 13
  *Exercise 1: How To Think Like a Poet* .................... 13
  *Exercise 2: How To Tell a Story* .............................. 15
  *Exercise 3: How To Dream in Color* ....................... 18
  *Exercise 4: List Poem* ............................................... 21
**How To Write a Poem With Rhymes** ........... 24
  *Exercise 5: How To Rhyme With Couplets* ........... 24
  *Exercise 6: How To Alternate Rhymes With Quatrains* .................................................................. 26
  *Exercise 7: How To Rhyme With The Sonnet* ....... 29
**How To Build Reading and Writing Skills** ... 33
  *1. Always Read!* ......................................................... 33
  *2. Always Write!* ........................................................ 34
**You're a Poet!** ............................................. 36
**Glossary** ..................................................... 37
**Recommended Resources** .......................... 39

# Introduction

If you're just starting out, writing poetry can seem difficult. Many people simply don't know how to start. However, learning how to write poetry is no different than learning how to do anything else, and can easily be learned with a little bit of practice and patience. And it doesn't all have to be about love or feelings. It can simply be a new way of looking at something familiar.

Writing poetry is an extremely rewarding experience, and has been practiced since the beginning of humanity. It is a means of communicating abstract ideas, telling stories, and seeing the world in fresh and interesting ways. And the best part of all is that it doesn't require any fancy equipment or expensive lessons.

This instructional handbook will guide you step by step through the process of becoming a poet. By the time you reach the end, you will be seeing the world in a whole new way, and will be writing poems every day and loving doing it.

## *Notes on How to Use This Guide*

Before taking on one of the exercises or activities in this guide, make sure you read all of the instructions over first. You should then read them again as you complete the activity.

This guide works best when you begin at the beginning and work to the end without skipping around. Don't skip over the beginning stuff! It's really important to your success as a poet.

After you've completed the course of this guide, don't be afraid to come back to it! You'll find that the information here will seem more and more useful every time you read it because you'll be bringing all that you've learned to the table.

There is a glossary at the end of this guide containing some definitions of poetic terminology used throughout. Enjoy!

# Tools Of The Trade

The first thing you need to do to write poetry is to collect the necessary tools to write. Luckily, they are all very inexpensive, and many people probably have them lying around their houses.

## 1. Select a Notebook

This may seem simple, but remember that this notebook will be very important to you, and you will be spending a lot of time using it. So, you should select one that is both sturdy and comfortable. Consider the following things when making your selection:

- ***Size:*** Your notebook should be portable, but big enough that you have room to write comfortable.
- ***Lined or Unlined:*** Some people prefer to "draw outside the lines" and work with unlined paper. Others prefer to organization of the lines. This is totally up to you.
- ***Soft or Hardcover:*** This is another matter of preference, but make sure that it will be both durable and comfortable enough for long term use.

Even if you prefer to type, keeping a notebook is a great way to be able to work anywhere at any time, no cords or batteries needed. You can still type up your poems later.

## *2. Select a Writing Implement*

Yes, this may seem like another no-brainer, but these are all necessary steps for writing poetry! And this is not as simple as you might think. You will quick find that you have a favorite pen or pencil, and won't leave home without it. Keep these things in mind as you try out various writing implements:

- ***Pen or Pencil:*** A few people like to use both, but most prefer one or the other. Some people like to erase, others like to cross out. Try out as many different types as you need to until you find the one that feels the best to you.
- ***Comfort:*** This is the most important quality. As you write poetry more and more, you will be writing for longer periods of time, and an uncomfortable pen can make this painful.
- ***Speed:*** Different types of pens and pencils write at different speeds. This is a matter of friction—the more friction, the slower the speed. Fountain pens tend to write fastest, and

sharp, hard graphite pencils tend to write slowest. Remember that faster is not always better. You want to be able to write as fast as you think, but also have good control.

## *3. Get a Dictionary & Thesaurus*

Because writing poetry is an art form in the medium of language, you'll need to be able to look up definitions of words you are unsure of to make sure you are using them properly. Likewise, a thesaurus (a book of synonyms, or words that mean the same thing) will come in handy when you need to find a word that is on the tip of your tongue but you can't get out. You should consider some or all of these options:

- **<u>PRINT DICTIONARY/THESAURUS:</u>** Although it might seem old fashioned, a good old paper dictionary or thesaurus is good to have for when you're not working at a computer. Also, you might see an interesting new word just flipping through the pages!
- **<u>ONLINE DICTIONARY:</u>** These days, this tool is absolutely indispensable for any writer or poet. Dictionary.com and Thesaurus.com are two great options for this.

- ***RHYMING DICTIONARY:*** These are in print and online as well. Not all poetry has to rhyme, but for when you need a rhyme, these tools can be wonderful.

## 4. Get a Poetry Anthology

Just like learning to play a sport, watching the professional and historical greats can be a fantastic asset to your progress. Your options here are diverse, so you can find the perfect one for you. Here are some things to consider as you select one (or ten!).

- ***ONLINE VERSIONS:*** Be careful of sites like Poetry.com that feature the work of other people who are still learning. You should be looking for the work of famous poets of past and present to learn from
- ***USED BOOKS:*** Thrift stores and used bookstores usually have dozens of poetry anthologies for a dollar or less. Most of them were only used as textbooks by one student, and are still as good as new!
- ***NEW BOOKS:*** If you order yours new, you will have the largest selection. This option is a little

more expensive, but you can still find plenty of reasonably priced poetry anthologies.

# How To Write a Poem

At this point you have all of the physical tools you need to be a poet. This is perhaps the best thing about writing, because so many other hobbies require that you shell out hundreds of dollars for equipment just to get started. But you have everything you need and more. The following section will provide you with some beginners writing exercises and tips.

## *Exercise 1: How To Think Like a Poet*

This exercise will help you to think and see the world in a new way. Being a poet is all about paying close attention to the world, and describing it in interesting ways.

Find any household object. This could literally be anything. A pencil, a mug, a book, a piece of paper—anything!

Look at it closely. Observe its color, its texture, its shape, its scent (maybe!). Think of things that it reminds you of. Really try and see it as if you've never seen it before. Even the most mundane objects are fascinating when viewed in a new way. Think of the places this object has been. Think of where it will go.

As you do this, make a list of words or phrases that come to your mind. Even single words like "white" or "big" are worth recording. Just write it all down. Do this for at least a few minutes.

Now write a poem about this object. The catch: you can't say what it is in the poem! It doesn't have to rhyme or have even line lengths. It may only be a few lines long (haiku only have three short lines!).

Your goal should be to describe this object in a way that no one has ever described it before. Use your list of words and phrases to help you as you write.

Now, use the name of the object as the title for the poem.

And you're done! You just wrote a poem! Some of the best and most famous poems in history were written just like this: people finding new ways to look at common things. In technical terms, this is called "defamiliarization," but you don't need to know that to achieve it!

### ***Example:***

Dollar bill: Creased, bent, green, pale green, ink, Washington, wrinkled, leaves, patterns, money, one, numbers, letters, pyramid, eagle, America, paper, smelly, been around, will leave me soon, temporary (your list may be much longer)

Little paper rectangle,

How many hands

Have you grown?

Leaves and vines spread

Outward and inward, holding

Value in a web

Of pale green pyramids,

Now wrinkled and faded.

Soon you will be gone.

*Your poem doesn't have to look like this. It can be any length, shape, or style you want. *You* are the artist! This goes for all the following exercises as well.

## *Exercise 2: How To Tell a Story*

Poetry that tells a story is called "narrative poetry" or "narrative verse." In this exercise, you will give it a try. It may sound silly or difficult, but it is neither!

Think of something that you do every day. Ideas might be: getting dressed, driving to work, doing the dishes, watching TV, exercising, etc.

Next time you do this activity, pay careful attention to the details of it. Constantly think of the action itself like a poem. If this activity was a poem, what would that poem be like?

Write down the sequence of events that occurs when you do this. (See the example if you're confused.)

Now, turn it into a poem! Make sure to describe it in a way that you've never thought of it before. You might utilize the list making practice from Exercise 1 to help get you going. Make the simple activity original and exciting. You can even write it in second person "You walk," third person "He or she walks," or first person "I walk."

All that's left to do is give it a title, and you've finished! This time, try to come up with a title that is only one word, but is not the action you are describing.

**_BONUS:_** Try to incorporate a simile or a metaphor into this poem.

A simile is the comparison of two unlike things using the words like or as. For example: "The sun is like a flower," or "The ships lined up like links in a chain."

A metaphor is the comparison of two unlike things *without using* the words like or as. For example: "The world is a battlefield," or "I'm on an island of loneliness."


### *Example:*

Getting the mail: First, I look at the clock and realize the mail should have come. Then I walk to the door, put on my shoes, open it, go onto the porch, open that door, walk out on the walkway, then across the driveway, then to the mail box, which is black and hangs from two chains. I open it and look inside, being careful to stay out of the road. I take the mail if there is any, close the mailbox, and retrace my steps inside.

Letters

It's four o'clock,

The winter sun is low

And snow

Glows and sparkles

He walks across

The cold floor

Creaking, like the door

Does as it opens.

Shoes slipped on

Like gloves, fitted

Loose and old.

The driveway is

Covered in snow.

The envelopes are

White and crisp

Like ice, as he returns

To the shoeless warmth

Of Saturday sleep

*You don't have to just write these just once! You can repeat an exercise many times, and in fact you should do this. Then you can compare your old and new work.

## *Exercise 3: How To Dream in Color*

Being a poet can be a lot like being a painter. You need to pay careful attention to color, and find new and innovative ways to describe it. In this exercise, you will work on viewing color like a painter and a poet, examining it closely and intensely.

Find a colorful picture. This can be from a magazine, the internet, a book of art, on your wall, etc. Just make sure you choose a picture with vibrant colors.

Make a list of the colors you see.

For each color, write down things that it reminds you of. You'll notice that there are many variations of each color, and that each one might remind you of something different.

Write a poem describing the picture, drawing from the pallet of colors and associations you've written down!

Give it a title, and you're finished! You can title it anything you want this time.

### ***Example:***

I'm looking at James Whistler's painting "The Falling Rocket."

Green: Like ocean water, or grass in the evening, but dirty with black mist. Algae, life, water.

Gold: Slightly tarnished jewelry, dull gold, bronzed, browning, like sand or clay. And pars of bright shining gold. Treasure. Value.

Black: Night sky, dark, speckled with white and pink and red.

Red: Fire, candy, cherry, fire engine, hot. Fireworks.

Pink: Cotton candy, pink sand, tongue speckles.

White: Like snow or smoke, dirty though, mingling with the black and green. Dusty. Clouds.

Ocean Treasure

Sky algae and ocean grass billow

And blend with the dust of smoke

And light, with grainy clouds of sand.

The red and pink fireworks fall

Like rainbow sprinkles, treasures

Gathered by the ocean, among the

Gold dust of sandy rust

The black ships are anchored

Volcanoes erupting

Candy and heat

In the noisy night air.

*You might consider writing numerous short poems, each about a certain color in the picture.

# *Exercise 4: List Poem*

So many great poems throughout history are simply lists. Of course, this doesn't mean your weekly grocery list is necessarily a poetic endeavor, but somehow list-based poems can seem easier to tackle sometimes. They're certainly easier to get started, anyway.

Come up with a theme or categories. This could be something like: colors, animals, flowers, fruits, anything! Just make sure it's something you know enough about to make a list based on it.

Make a list of things in this category. This list could be a short as three things, or as long as you'd like. Try to keep it reasonable though. Or else you may find yourself unable to finish the poem you'll be writing from it.

On a new sheet of paper (or in a new program window if you're typing), write a poem based on this list. The poem itself will be the list, actually. But for each item, you'll need to elaborate in a descriptive way.

Try to have all of these items come together to form a single, cohesive unit of poetry.

You may want to go back and add an introduction to the poem, and you want to make some concluding remarks, in order to make the poem work as a whole.

**BONUS:** Try to incorporate alliteration into this poem. Alliteration is when you repeat the sound at the beginning of words, like ruby red racecar, or big blue baseball, or Great Gatsby. This can be a lot of fun, and is a technique that many poets use. You can just have two words with the same sound, or many in a row.

Can you spot the alliteration in the example poem?

Things of my desk: Coffee cup, notebook, laptop, lamp, cell phone, envelopes, pen.

My coffee cup

Contains cold

Caffeine and cream

Which spilled on to

My notebook, staining

My poetry.

The laptop is cold

Too, and holds

Nothing but wires.

The luminous lamp light

Pours watts of white

And red heat onto my hands

As the cell phone rings

And I put my head in my hands

And feel endlessly tired.

Empty envelopes

Hold hope, like

Dream clouds.

If only my pen knew

Where to send their

Fragile frames

Then all would be right

In the world.

*If you decide to write a long one, try a short one after. Choose just three objects.

# How To Write a Poem With Rhymes

Many people think all poetry has to rhyme at the end of lines, but that couldn't be further from the truth. In fact, most contemporary poetry doesn't rhyme at all. However, rhyming can be a lot of fun, even if you only include a rhyme or two in a poem.

Writing good rhyming poetry also requires a lot of practice. At first, you might find it hard to find good rhymes. Practice will make this easier, and by the time you finish these exercises, you'll be a rhyming expert!

## *Exercise 5: How To Rhyme With Couplets*

To practice rhyming, you will be using couplet, which are lines grouped in twos. To make rhymes work best, it helps if you use the same number of syllables in each line. For this practice, you will be using four syllables in each line. This will likely be a sort of silly, simple poem. So have fun with it!

Write a line about yourself with four syllables. It could be about your appearance, your personality, your likes and dislikes, whatever you want.

Next, write another line that talks about the same quality you wrote in the first. This could be a response to it, or a qualification of some kind. (See the example if you're confused.) Any make sure the last syllable rhymes with the first line

Leave a space and do it again! This time, make sure you have a different rhyming sound at the end.

Try to do this for four couplets.

After finishing four, you can certainly continue if you'd like.

Give it a title, and you're all done.

If you can't come up with a perfect rhyme, that's fine. Try finding a word that almost rhymes. This is called a "slant rhyme."

### ***Example:***

Self Portrait

My hair is brown

I rarely frown

My coffee's black

My mug is cracked

I like to hike

And sometimes bike

My eyes are green

But they're not mean

I'll write a poem

And read a tome

And play guitar

You'll hear from far

I love the sea

And cherry trees

But not the pits

Or oven mitts

So, this is me

I do decree!

*Remember to have fun with this! It doesn't have to make perfect sense. As long as you try to rhyme, it will be great practice.

## *Exercise 6: How To Alternate Rhymes With Quatrains*

Next in your rhyming practice, you'll be trying quatrains. These are groups of four lines, like two couplets put together. You should have 10 syllables in each line this time!

For this poem you can write about anything. If you're having trouble coming up with a topic, you can write about yourself like you did in the last exercise. You might also consider writing about nature, your everyday life, or things that you love. It's completely up to you.

The rhyme scheme you'll be using is ABAB CDCD.

A rhyme scheme is a way of keeping track of which lines rhyme with which.

In this exercise, the first and third lines of each quatrain will rhyme, and so will the second and fourth. But the different quatrains don't need to rhyme with each other.

This mixing up of rhymes is called "alternating rhymes."

Don't forget to count your syllables to make sure there are ten in each line.

Counting by tapping your fingers helps. Go through your five fingers twice!

If you're off by a syllable but it stills sound right to your ear, then it's okay.

After you complete two quatrains you can stop, find a title, and you're done.

If you want to write more quatrains, don't hesitate!

### ***Example:***

The sun is rising out over the lawn

My eyes are heavy, but I've got to rise

I walk to the window with a heavy yawn

And rub the sand out of my morning eyes

The robins fly around looking for food

I think of coffee and I smile wide

The thought of breakfast lightens up my mood

I think of having eggs scrambled or fried

*Not all poems have to be about serious subjects or emotions. Light hearted or funny poems are called "light verse," and can be a lot of fun to read and write.

# *Exercise 7: How To Rhyme With The Sonnet*

While many people have heard of a sonnet and know that William Shakespeare wrote them, very few people actually know what make a sonnet a sonnet. Here, you will learn its characteristics, and even try writing one yourself.

Be warned, this is the most difficult exercise in the guide, and it will take some time to do. Don't get down if you need to write it many times to figure it out. This is completely normal.

**The Characteristics of a Sonnet**

While there are a few different types of sonnets, the one we will be looking at now is the Shakespearian sonnet.

**A Shakespearian sonnet has:**

14 lines grouped into 4 parts

Three groups of four lines (called quatrains)

One group of two lines (called a couplet)

Ten syllables in each line

(A, B, A, B,) (C, D, C, D,) (E, F, E, F,) (G, G,) Rhyme Scheme (I'll explain)

**The Rhyme Scheme**

Each letter corresponds to the sound at the end of each line. So, the first and third lines rhyme, and so do the second and fourth, the fifth and seventh, the sixth and eighth, the seventh and ninth, plus the tenth and twelfth. Then, the final two lines, number thirteen and fourteen, rhyme as well. If you are having a hard time with this, look up some sonnets online to get an idea of how this rhyming works.

In the tradition of sonnet writing, you will be writing a love sonnet, just like Shakespeare!

Think of something or someone that you love. This could be a significant other, a pet, a family member, a favorite food, anything! Contemporary poets have written love poems to everything from dogs to a favorite pair of shoes!

Make a list of associations that you have with this love, just like you did for the first exercise.

Write a sonnet about it!

**Things to be careful of as you write your sonnet:**

Make sure you count your syllables! This is a very difficult practice, and if you are one syllable off here and there, don't worry about it. Even Shakespeare wasn't perfect.

Remember to pay attention to your rhymes. Don't choose end words that are hard to rhyme with. You'll probably find that you have to go back and change a word sometimes to make a rhyme work.

Don't be afraid to mix some sadness into the sonnet too. Mixing joy and despair is a mark of a great poet.

Have fun! Don't get too frustrated with it. If it's not working out, you can always start over. They get easier to write every time.

### *Example:*

My favorite spot to write, out by the pond. Springtime, bees, flowers. Clear skies. No roads or walk ways. All clear and pleasant. But also, the sadness of not being able to go there often enough, because I'm stuck in my car or going to work or the store. Concrete paths. Nature. Beauty.

### The Pond

Clear as the wind-swept sky it seems to me

That I should find my tranquil pond among

Dead leaves, living grass, and striped bumblebees

Which feed on the nectar sweet to my tongue;

And not along false concrete paths, laden

With such worthless things, valued less than dirt.

Still—I walk them with strides, singing cadence

Of all my longings, sickness, hate, and hurt.

I wonder when, if ever, I shall trade

Oil-stained puddles for that tranquil pond:

The wicked, wretched mess humans have made

For something real and pure, spawned from beyond.

Perhaps not until when in death I lay,

Becoming that to which I longed to stray.

\*Note that you don't have to leave spaces between the segments. It's up to you, and different poets have done it different ways. It's just a matter of personal preference.

# How To Build Reading and Writing Skills

Becoming a good poet takes more than just writing poetry. You have to hone your abilities to use language in new ways, and to experience words in an expert way, with a fresh light. But this isn't really work. Chances are you'll find these activities extremely enjoyable and enriching, and will be proud to pursue them and share what you learn with others.

## *1. Always Read!*

It is important that you always remember to read from your poetry anthologies. You won't like all of the poem, you won't understand them all, either. And that's okay! Just look for the ones you like. You should read poetry as often as you can, every day if possible. Here are some things to do to keep you reading and looking for new poems:

- **<u>SHARE WITH A FRIEND:</u>** If you find a poem you love, share it with a friend or family member. Chances are they'll enjoy it too, and be impressed with you! It can also be a great opportunity to show a loved one how you feel with someone else's words.
- **<u>CUT AND PASTE:</u>** You might consider cutting out favorite poems and putting them on your

bulletin board or even your refrigerator. They will serve as constant reminders to thin poetically. Posting poems on social networking site like facebook.com is also a great idea.

- ***TAKE A CLASS:*** Local libraries and colleges often offer survey courses in poetry. These courses would be of great help on your journey to becoming a poet.
- ***ASK YOUR FRIENDS:*** Even if you don't think they are in to poetry, a lot of people have a favorite poem they would lot to share with you.
- ***READ NOVELS:*** Believe it or not, reading your favorite novels will help you become a better poet. Now that you brain is trained to think like a poet, you will be reading books in a whole new way, constantly building your vocabulary and poetic instincts.

## *2. Always Write!*

To become a poet is to become a writer. This means that all sort of writing will improve your ability as a poet. Here are some good ways to keep you writing every day, even if it's not poetry:

- ***KEEP A DAILY JOURNAL:*** It doesn't much matter what you write about or how much you write, what's important is that you are writing—turning ideas into word on paper or a computer screen. Also, you will find that as you recall things about your day, you will remember beautiful little details and then be inspired to write a poem about it.
- ***KEEP A DREAM JOURNAL:*** This can go along with you daily journal, and will serve for excellent poetry fodder! You might consider keeping this in a notebook or on one of the many online journal sites.
- ***WRITE LETTERS:*** This might seem old fashioned, but writing letters by hand or on the computer will help to hone your writing abilities. E-mails work great too. And while you're writing these letters, you can always share your interest in poetry with family and friends.

# You're a Poet!

If you've completed this book, you are officially a poet! To be a poet, all you need to do is to continue to write poetry. Don't let your notebook gather dust! Also read and write, and never stop learning.

You should be proud of the poetic accomplishments you've already made, and you should share them with the people in your life. Although it's fine to keep your poetry to yourself (do a search on Emily Dickenson), sharing it can be just as rewarding as writing it.

Good luck with your future writing, and never forget to look at the world in new and exciting ways every day of your life!

# Glossary

**_ALLITERATION:_** The technique of repeating the sound at the beginning of words, like ruby red racecar.

**_ALTERNATING RHYME:_** When rhyme sounds alternate from line to line. See *Rhyme Scheme* for information on this.

**_ANTHOLOGY:_** A book that is a collection of work by many different writers. Anthologies are usually categorized by style or time period.

**_COUPLET:_** A group of two lines. If they rhyme, they are called a "rhyming couplet."

**_DEFAMILIARIZATION:_** The effect of taking something familiar and making it seem unfamiliar by presenting it in a new way.

**_RHYME:_** When the end of two or more words has the same sound, like meeker beaker, or round ground.

**_RHYME SCHEME:_** The organization of a pattern for rhyming in a poem. This is usually represented by a lettering system, like ABAB, where A rhymes with A and B rhymes with B.

**_LIGHT VERSE:_** The term for poems that are light hearted or funny.

**_METAPHOR:_** The comparison of two unlike things *without using* the words like or as. For example: "The world is a battlefield," or "I'm on an island of loneliness." Similar to a simile.

***NARRATIVE VERSE:*** This is a type of poem that tells a story. This type of poetry "narrates" a series of events, much like a fictional short story.

***QUATRAIN:*** A group of four lines. The lines can be different lengths, and can rhyme or not rhyme.

***SIMILE:*** The comparison of two unlike things *using* the words like or as. For example: "The sun is like a flower," or "The ships lined up like links in a chain."

***SLANT RHYME:*** Like a rhyme, except the words don't end with exactly the same sound. Some examples are black and cracked, purse and burst, or rhyme and hind.

***SONNET:*** A form of poetry using 14 lines with 10 syllables each. The standard rhyme scheme is ABAB CDCD EFEF GG. William Shakespeare commonly used the sonnet.

***VERSE:*** Another word for poetry. It comes from the use of the word verse in music.

# Recommended Resources

- HowExpert.com – Quick 'How To' Guides on All Topics from A to Z by Everyday Experts.
- HowExpert.com/free – Free HowExpert Email Newsletter.
- HowExpert.com/books – HowExpert Books
- HowExpert.com/courses – HowExpert Courses
- HowExpert.com/clothing – HowExpert Clothing
- HowExpert.com/membership – HowExpert Membership Site
- HowExpert.com/affiliates – HowExpert Affiliate Program
- HowExpert.com/writers – Write About Your #1 Passion/Knowledge/Expertise & Become a HowExpert Author.
- HowExpert.com/resources – Additional HowExpert Recommended Resources
- YouTube.com/HowExpert – Subscribe to HowExpert YouTube.
- Instagram.com/HowExpert – Follow HowExpert on Instagram.
- Facebook.com/HowExpert – Follow HowExpert on Facebook.

Printed in Great Britain
by Amazon